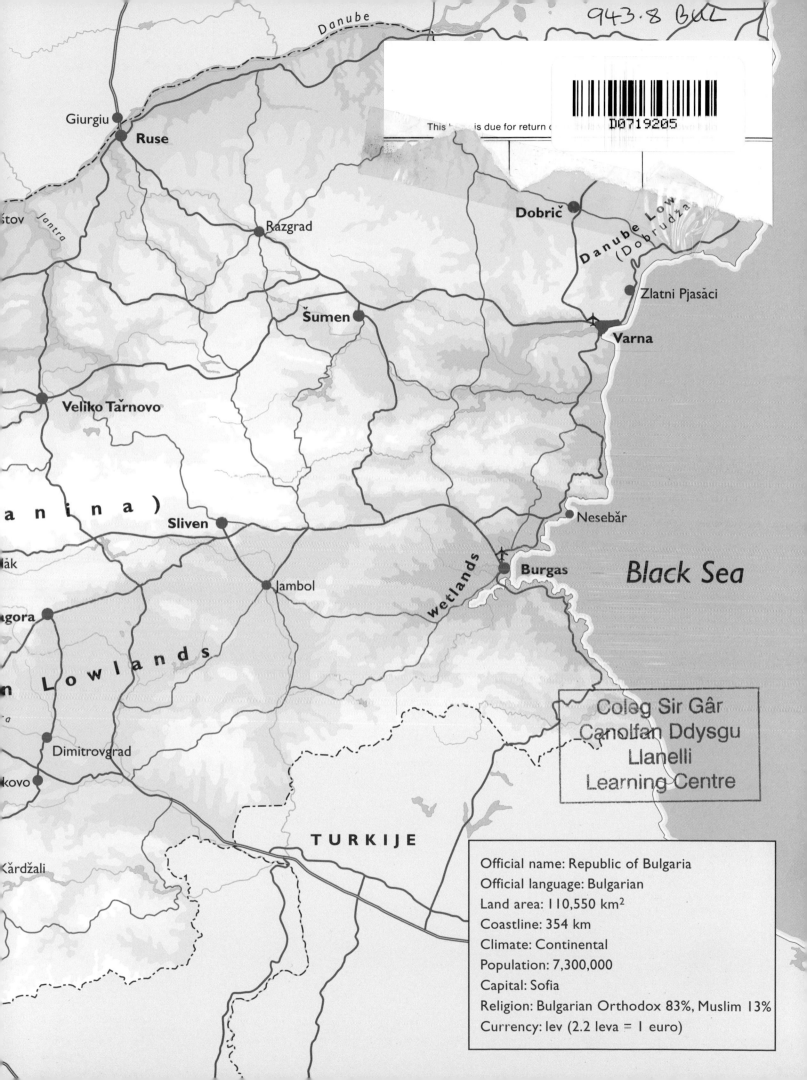

Danube

Giurgiu

Ruse

štov

Jantra

Razgrad

Dobrič

Danube Low (Dobrudža

Zlatni Pjasáci

Šumen

Varna

Veliko Tǎrnovo

anina)

Sliven

Nesebǎr

äk

Wetlands

Jambol

Burgas

Black Sea

agora

Lowlands

a

Dimitrovgrad

kovo

TURKIJE

Kǎrdžali

Official name: Republic of Bulgaria
Official language: Bulgarian
Land area: 110,550 km²
Coastline: 354 km
Climate: Continental
Population: 7,300,000
Capital: Sofia
Religion: Bulgarian Orthodox 83%, Muslim 13%
Currency: lev (2.2 leva = 1 euro)

New EU Countries and Citizens

Bulgaria

Bronja Prazdny

▶ *The Bojana Church in Sofia dates from the eleventh century. Its famous murals were painted in 1259.*

The First Bulgarian Empire lasted until 1018, when it was once again absorbed by the Byzantine Empire. For many years the Bulgarians tried to rid themselves of their overlords and finally managed to do so in 1185. In that year, two Bulgarian *bojars* (landowners), Petar and Asen, led a successful revolt against the Byzantines, marking the beginning of the Second Bulgarian Empire. Veliko Tarnovo became the new capital city. Petar and Asen's youngest brother, Tsar Kalojan, also managed to regain some land from the Byzantines, but Bulgaria was still not as large as it had once been. The surrounding countries had grown too strong for the Bulgarians to fight them.

At the start of the Second Bulgarian Empire, the economy, trade and Bulgarian culture all flourished. However, the *bojars* began to fight among themselves and the internal conflicts caused the power of the empire to decline. A weakened Bulgaria proved no match for the advancing Ottoman Turks, and in 1393 they invaded and occupied Veliko Tarnovo. Within a few years, the Ottomans had conquered the whole of Bulgaria.

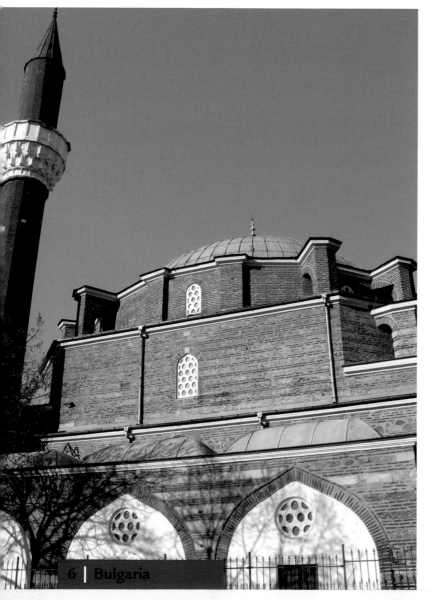

Five centuries of Turkish rule

Life was difficult for Bulgarians under the rule of the Turkish sultans. They had to pay high taxes to their foreign overlords, which forced many of them into poverty. The Bulgarian people also suffered from the cruelty and corruption of local and provincial officials as well as the abuse of power by the clergy. The Turkish sultan had removed many Bulgarians from positions of authority, particularly in the Church. All Orthodox (Byzantine) churches became subject to rule from the Church in the Turkish capital of Constantinople.

Although Islam was not immediately proclaimed as the state religion, only Muslims could occupy high positions, causing many Bulgarian noblemen to convert from Christianity to Islam. Most ordinary people remained loyal to the Orthodox Church, although this was not always easy. During the 500 years they were ruled by the Ottomans, life remained hard for ordinary people. Many of the changes that swept through Europe in these five centuries simply passed by Bulgaria.

◀ *The Banja Baši Mosque (1576) is one of the oldest in Europe and the only mosque still in use in Sofia. Banja Baši means 'washing a lot'.*

On a bitterly cold November day in Sofia town centre, Eva catches her breath in Slavejkov Square. 'There's plenty of room beside these two gentlemen,' she explains, sitting on the bench beside the statues of Petko Slavejkov and his son Penco. The square is named after these two nineteenth-century poets. Petko Slavejkov was a famous Bulgarian writer, who penned many poems and articles encouraging his compatriots to fight for independence from Ottoman rule in their country.

It was not until the nineteenth century that commercial and cultural ties with Western countries started to develop, thanks to the forward-thinking Sultan Abdulmejitt. He wanted to transform the Ottoman Empire into a modern (Western) state, and to end religious discrimination within the empire. The Bulgarians took the opportunity to demand their own church, free of the Patriarchate of Constantinople. There was strong resistance to this, but in 1870 the sultan declared the establishment of an independent Bulgarian Church.

▲ The ceiling of the fifteenth-century Trojan Monastery in the Stara Planina Mountains. Vasil Levski often visited here.

Vasil Levski was born in 1837 in the town of Karlovo in what was then the Ottoman Empire. His real name was Vasil Ivanov Kuncev. Levski means 'lion-like' and he earned this nickname because of a great jump he made during a military exercise, when his friends said he looked just like a lion. Levski was committed to the cause of Bulgarian independence. A network of revolutionary groups was set up under his leadership, all of them in contact with each other. They carried out violent campaigns against Ottoman officials. In 1872, Levski was arrested and the following year he was hanged by the Turks. However, the revolutionary committees remained active even after his death. They organised the April Revolt of 1876, and although this was unsuccessful it instigated the Turco-Russian War, which eventually led to a free and independent Bulgaria.

Striving for independence

The fight for independence began to gain ground in the nineteenth century, and a Bulgarian propaganda machine evolved. Great historical battles in Bulgaria were praised, Bulgarian heroes of the past were honoured and Bulgaria's own language and religion were celebrated. Besides the call for more cultural individuality there were also people who wanted a radical break with the Ottomans. One of the pioneers of this freedom movement was Vasil Levski (see panel).

◀ Vasil Levski, a hero in the fight for Bulgarian independence.

Mountain ranges

The Stara Planina, or the Balkan Range, lies in southern Bulgaria. This massive mountain range runs right through the country from the Black Sea in the east to Sofia and then to the north-west. It crosses the border into Romania, where it meets the Carpathians.

The Sredna Gora range lies close to the Stara Planina. It covers around 600 km and forms a natural barrier, dividing Bulgaria in half. This mountain range consists of three regions: the High Balkan in the north and the West and East Balkans. The highest peak in the High Balkan is Botev, at 2,390 m.

The Thracian Lowlands lie south of the Balkan Mountains. This fertile, hilly area is good for agriculture. Another mountain range lies in the south-west of the country. It is made up of three geological formations known as massifs: the Rila and the Pirin Mountains, and in the south the Rodopi Massif, which stretches into Greece. The highest peak in Bulgaria is the Musala, in the Rila Range, which is 2,925 m high. This mountain was named *Moes-Allah*, which means 'Allah's mountain', by the Ottomans during the period of Turkish rule.

High in the mountains, above the tree line, there are only bare rocks and a few small mountain lakes. However, the lower-lying mountains, especially the Rodopi Massif, are very green. Here lie rough forests and alpine meadows covered with unusual flowers, such as the rare and protected edelweiss. It is a popular area for hiking.

▶ *The Rajsko Praskalo ('Heavenly Mist') in winter.*

South of the capital, Sofia, lies Mount Vitoša (1,843 m). It can be seen from the city. Even though it is little more than a large, dome-shaped clump of stones – certainly not one of Bulgaria's most beautiful features – it is still worth climbing, if only to escape the smog of the capital. The northern mountainside is wooded. Vitoša was created during a volcanic eruption.

The coastal plain in eastern Bulgaria is the lowest part of the country. The northern region of the plain – with the town of Varna as its focal point – is rugged and rocky with red cliffs. To the south there are a lot of small, rocky bays with Mediterranean overgrowth. Burgas is the biggest town here.

One-third of Bulgaria consists of high mountain ranges, one-third is settled with towns and cities, and the remaining third is grassland and low mountains with vineyards.

Rivers and lakes

There are 526 rivers in Bulgaria. All the rivers north of the Balkan Mountains flow into the Danube and then into the Black Sea. All the rivers south of this mountain range flow into the Aegean Sea. A few small rivers in the east of the country flow directly into the Black Sea. Only the Danube, which marks Bulgaria's border with Romania, is navigable. After the Volga, the Danube is the longest river in Europe. The Iskăr (370 km) is the longest river in Bulgaria, rising in Lake Čamovsko at a height of 2,515 m in the Rila Mountains. From there it flows through the eastern suburbs of Sofia and through the Balkan Mountains into the Danube.

▲ A stream in the Rila Mountains.

▼ The 'Lake of Fish', one of the Rila Lakes.

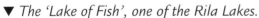

Glacier lakes were formed from melting glaciers at the end of the last ice age. Bulgaria has about 200 glacier lakes, many of them high in the Rila and Pirin Mountains. In the Rila range there are nearly 150 glacier lakes, the highest of which lies at about 2,716 m. The seven Rila Lakes are the most beautiful, and they are a popular tourist destination. The highest of these seven is the Salzăta Ezero, known as the 'Lake of Tears'. Its waters are so clear that it is possible see the bottom of the lake. Lake Okoto, which means 'the eye', was given this name because it is nearly a perfect oval. It is 37 m deep.

Climate

Bulgaria has a moderate continental climate, with cold winters and hot summers. The north has a real continental climate, with very cold winters and long, hot summers. The Balkan Mountains and the Black Sea greatly influence the weather. South of the Balkan Mountains the weather is less dramatic because these mountains form a natural barrier. Closer to Greece, the country becomes more Mediterranean in climate. In summer the temperature here can rise considerably, especially along the coast. Fortunately, the sea breeze reduces these high temperatures. Annual rainfall in Bulgaria is 50 to 70 mm, but in the mountains the average is more than 100 mm, and it often falls as snow. The roads through the mountain passes can become blocked with snow and impassable to traffic.

National symbols

The Bulgarian flag has three horizontal stripes: white, green and red. The white stands for peace, the green for nature, and the red for the blood spilt over the centuries.

The Bulgarian national anthem is called *Mila Rodino* ('Beloved Fatherland'). In 1964 this became the official anthem, but the words have changed over the years, including in 1990 when the communist era came to an end.

The Bulgarian currency is the Lev. One Lev is 100 Stotinki. There are two Leva to one Euro. There are a lot of fake banknotes in circulation in Bulgaria, especially 20-Leva notes. If a banknote's watermark shows the Bulgarian lion, it is a real one. Bulgaria plans to adopt the Euro in 2010.

The name 'Balkan' can refer to both the peninsula in south-eastern Europe and the mountain range that runs right through Bulgaria. Today, the word has negative connotations, because all the wars in the region have been known as the Balkan Wars, so the name is often equated with conflict. Bulgarians prefer to speak of South-east Europe – the region that consists of Bulgaria, Greece, Serbia, Macedonia, Bosnia-Herzegovina, Montenegro and Albania. All these countries were ruled by the Ottomans in the past. Croatia, Slovenia, Romania and the European part of Turkey are also considered part of the Balkans by some people.

Bulgarians think of the Balkan Mountains as the true symbol of their country. They call them the Stara Planina, which means 'Old Mountain'. Balkan is Turkish for 'Forested Mountain'. Bulgarians celebrate their mountains in poems, stories and songs – and it is the first thing mentioned in the national anthem.

◄ *A 10-Leva banknote with with a picture of Dr Peter Beron (1799–1871), scientist and language moderniser.*

Cities

In recent years, many Bulgarians have moved from the countryside to the cities in search of work and better facilities such as healthcare.

In 1900 only 20 per cent of the Bulgarian population lived in towns and cities. Today, 72 per cent live in towns and only 28 per cent in rural areas. The capital, Sofia, is the most populated city, with more than 1.2 million inhabitants.

Sofia

The number of people living in Sofia has increased dramatically since the end of the nineteenth century. In 1887 the city had only 21,000 inhabitants. Thirteen years later there were 47,000 and in 1946 more than half a million people lived in the capital. In 2007 this number had more than doubled. The population density in Sofia is about 600 people per km². This is not very high when compared to a city like London, which has a population density of 4,700 people per km².

▲ Apartments in Sofia.

▲ Book stalls on Slavejkov Square.

Sofia lies in the western part of the country, at the foot of Mount Vitoša, and at weekends, many people who live in the city enjoy hiking up the mountain. Sofia is the seat of the Bulgarian government and the home of the president. Many international companies have their headquarters in Sofia and the stock exchange is based there. Sofia is also a university city, with 17 universities and colleges.

The city has good public transport, with an underground railway, buses, trams and trolley buses. Tickets can be bought at the station, and travellers stamp them themselves using the machines on the tram or bus. A ticket costs about 20 pence.

◀ Count Ignatiev Street in the centre of Sofia.

At last – just the two of us....

This couple are enjoying a summer's day in each other's company. Quietly they look over the town of Plovdiv, which lies at their feet. The view from this mountain – one of the six in the province of Plovdiv – is breathtaking. They have decided to sit high up here to enjoy the peace and quiet.

After Sofia, Plovdiv is the most important cultural and tourist centre in Bulgaria. The old town centre is particularly beautiful, with small, cobbled streets leading up a steep slope. Both sides of the street are lined with traditional houses in 'Bulgarian renaissance' style, dating from the nineteenth century. The streets are named after the rich merchants and noblemen who once occupied this part of the town, although many of the houses have now been converted into museums or restaurants.

The port of Varna

The port town of Varna is situated on the coast, and is known as the 'Pearl of the Black Sea'. This is Bulgaria's third-largest town, and has a population of about 325,000. The town and the nearby beaches are very popular with tourists. In 2006 more than 4.7 million people visited Varna, nearly four million of them from overseas. About 20 km north of Varna are the well-known Zlatni Pjasăci, or 'Golden Sands'. This is a long stretch of beach with many hotels, restaurants and cafés.

▲ *A small street in Plovdiv.*

Varna is home to many treasures from different periods in Bulgarian history, including thermal baths that date from the third century, when the Romans ruled the area. Parts of these gigantic excavations can be seen in the town, in the streets and even in between houses. Some parts of the baths are still buried beneath the town.

▶ *The cathedral at Varna dates from 1886.*

The Sea Gardens is a large park that runs parallel to the coast. Built at the beginning of the twentieth century, the gardens contain an aquarium, a dolphin park, a planetarium, several museums, a small zoo and a children's park full of attractions. Many unusual plants and flowers can also be seen here, as well as plenty of statues.

▲ *Varna beach*

Burgas – the festival city

The second-largest town on the Black Sea – and the fourth-largest in Bulgaria – is Burgas, which has a population of 195,000. It lies on the most westerly point of the Bay of Burgas, on a peninsula surrounded by three natural lakes, swamps and protected nature reserves (wetlands). People come here for bird-watching, as several rare species can be seen. Burgas is very popular with tourists. It is surrounded by breathtaking countryside, and there are many hotels, restaurants and cafés. The area has a warm climate and a relaxed atmosphere, as well as plenty to see and do. The dark-sand beach can be reached by a spiral staircase. Each year, at the end of August, an International Folklore Festival takes place in the Park on the Sea; this festival has been held here for more than 35 years.

The port at Burgas is smaller than the one at Varna but more cargo passes through it. Nearly three-quarters of Bulgaria's imports and exports go through Burgas, and the harbour provides an important source of income for the town.

Ruse

Ruse lies in the north, on the right bank of the Danube, and is an important inland port. It has 160,000 inhabitants and is the country's fifth-largest town. Across the river is Romania. From here it is possible to take a ferry to the Romanian town of Giurgiu and the Ukrainian port of Reni. Ruse is the cultural and economic heart of the north. The architecture here is typically European, and walking through the town, one can see similarities with Paris or Vienna.

▲ *The Danube.*

Among the best-known of Ruse's 200 or so important historical buildings is Dochodnoto Zdanie ('the profitable building'). This old theatre, dating from 1902, has a statue of Mercury, the winged god of commerce, on the roof. Together with the Liberty Monument, built in 1908, this statue has become a symbol of the town

▶ *Visitors enjoy strolling through the streets of Ruse.*

Transport

Bulgaria lies in an important position in Europe, and many large roads connecting other European countries with parts of the Middle East criss-cross the country.

▲ *Many people in Bulgaria have unreliable cars.*

Bulgaria has an extensive and dense network of roads, totalling 40,234 km. Although 90 per cent of the roads are paved, only around 400 km of the road network is motorway. The rest is made up of small, local roads so traffic jams are common and journeys can take a long time.

Road safety

Many roads in Bulgaria are not well-maintained – falling far below the standards of countries in Western Europe. They are littered with cracks and potholes, and few of them are well-lit, so driving at night can be dangerous. To make matters worse, Bulgarians often drive without their lights on, so road accidents are not uncommon. There are a lot of horses and carts on Bulgaria's roads – on both large and small roads, in the towns as well as the countryside. When driving in Bulgaria, it is important to remember all these hazards and be prepared!

Sometimes even in October, snow can be a nuisance. Many smaller roads are already in poor condition, but when it snows they are nearly impassable. Small mountain villages are often cut off from the outside world because mountain passes are snowed under in winter. Because many Bulgarians have old cars, driving in winter can be dangerous.

◀ *Bulgaria's roads can be dangerous for careless drivers.*

▼ *Goods being transported by rail.*

Improving the infrastructure

Improving Bulgaria's road network requires a lot of money, but the EU has started granting subsidies to help repair them, and they are slowly improving. In 2006, the Bulgarian government promised to spend more than £10 billion over the following 10 years to improve the road infrastructure in Bulgaria, making motorways a priority.

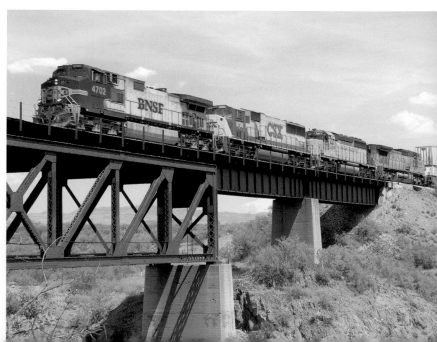

► *These men work on the railways; they think rail links should be improved across Bulgaria.*

Despite this investment, more projects are needed to bring Bulgaria in line with standards elsewhere in Europe. Train connections within the country and with neighbouring countries must be improved. A second bridge needs to be built across the Danube to Romania. In 2006, Sofia airport was improved and extended, and other airports should be renovated in the same way. Although there are many building projects underway, some of them have been put on hold because of lack of money.

◄ *Tram and trolley bus.*

Public transport

Public transport is affordable, connections are reasonable and services usually run on time. The problem is that – just as with the roads – too many buses, trams and, in particular, trains, are very old and need to be replaced. Most people travel by bus and there are bus connections to around 90 per cent of populated areas in Bulgaria. Only high mountain villages are not on a bus route. Although travelling by bus is usually fast and reliable, not all bus companies offer the same standards of service – some buses are quite clean and pleasant, others are extremely old and look as if they have never been cleaned.

▲ *This sign reads: 'Children have no brakes!'*

In Sofia, around 85 per cent of the working population takes the bus to their job. Many children also take the bus to school – if they don't walk. An alternative is the trolley bus, which runs on electricity from overhead wires. There is an underground rail system in Sofia, but it only runs for around 10 km. There are plans to extend this underground system to to 50 km, with around 30 stations.

Dimitar and his father Kamen are rag-and-bone men. It's a meagre existence and they must work hard to earn enough money to survive. They rely on their old horse to haul them and their cart around. They're on their way to their junkyard, where this Volkswagen Beetle will be stripped down to separate any useful parts. Dimitar and his father will then sell these, and the steel from the casing.

▶ *The port at Varna.*

Shipping

There are five important ports in Bulgaria. Varna and Burgas, on the Black Sea, are important for the storage and warehousing of goods between Europe and the Middle East. As well as these two seaports, there are three inland ports along the Danube. The one at Ruse is the largest, and accounts for two-thirds of all inland shipping in the country. The other harbours are near Lom and Vidin. The EU is providing money to improve navigation on the Danube and to expand and modernise the inland ports.

In May 2007 approval was granted to start building a second bridge along the Danube frontier. It will lie between Calafat in Romania and Vidin in Bulgaria. The bridge will be an important link between the Balkan countries and Central and Western Europe. It is being financed with money from the European Union and a number of European banks. It will be nearly 2 km long, with four lanes for cars and a railway line. It was hoped that work would be completed in 2010, making it possible to cross from Bulgaria to Romania in three ways – by car, rail or ferry. However, the project is currently running low on funding, and corruption and poor organisation means that completing this large construction project may take longer than hoped.

There is only one bridge over the Danube between Bulgaria and Romania, the Friendship Bridge, which stretches between Ruse and Giurgiu in Romania. It is nearly 3.2 km long and was built in 1954.

Ferries

It is possible to take a ferry from Varna across the Black Sea to two towns in the Ukraine and one in Georgia. There is also a ferry service from Burgas to Odessa in the Ukraine, and several places where a ferry runs across the Danube to Romania. A trip from Vidin to Calafat takes about 20 minutes, but the ferry only leaves when it's full – which means that passengers can sometimes have a long wait.

Air travel

The national airline, Bulgaria Air, was established in 2002, after the previous airline – Balkan Bulgarian Airlines – ceased to exist. The fleet now consists of 11 aircraft: all Boeing 737s. The three international airports lie near Sofia, Varna and Burgas. Varždebna near Sofia accounts for nearly 37 per cent of all passengers. In 2006 this airport was renovated and enlarged; a second runway and a new terminal were added. The airports of Varna and Burgas must also be expanded if Bulgaria is to improve its air transport. The airports in Plovdiv and Gerna Orjachovica are used mainly for freight.

▼ *Vrazdebna airport in Sofia has been expanded and modernised.*

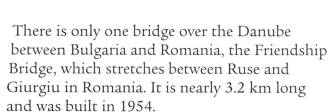

People

More than 7.3 million people live in Bulgaria, and about 84 per cent of these are of Bulgarian descent.

◀ *A school outing in the town of Levski.*

Because of its difficult history, Bulgarian society often stereotypes people, and Bulgarians can be prejudiced against minorities, asylum seekers and refugees. It is not uncommon to see foreigners abused or to hear Bulgaria's problems blamed on 'the Turks'. The media – newspapers, magazines and television – makes this problem worse by using hate language and racial slurs, and by encouraging intolerance of foreigners in Bulgaria. Since Bulgaria became a member of the EU, however, this behaviour has become less common.

Turks are the largest of the minority groups (about 9.5 per cent) in Bulgaria, followed by the Roma, or Gypsies. There are believed to be between 350,000 and 800,000 Roma in the country. The rest of the population is made up of small groups of Russians, Armenians, Vlachs, Macedonians, Greeks and some Ukrainians, Romanians and Jews.

Roma

The Roma people suffer most from prejudice and discrimination in Bulgaria. This may be a reason why there are no exact figures of how many Roma there are in the country – people are afraid to admit that they belong to this group. Living conditions for the Roma are often poor. Many of them live crowded together in slums that are dangerous and badly maintained. Rubbish is often left uncollected and there is no electricity. The drains often leak. Usually the Roma have no access to healthcare. They are very poor and have no health insurance because most of them are unemployed.

◀▲ *Roma people play music on a train to Bansko. Having played a piece, they pass the hat round, hoping that people will give them some money. Then they move on to the next carriage.*

Many Roma can't read well because they left school at a young age. The Bulgarians often blame the Roma for crime – if there is a burglary, for example, others will look immediately to the Roma in the community, and hold them responsible.

Shrinking population

Since 1990 the Bulgarian population has been shrinking by about 1 per cent a year because more people die than are born. Life expectancy is also low: on average, men only reach the age of 68.5 years old and women about 76 years. The low birth rate (about 1.4 children per woman) is leading to a reduction in population and is caused by poor healthcare, bad eating habits, poverty and a low standard of living. The infant mortality rate is very high – more than three times that in the United Kingdom.

◄ *If Bulgaria's low birth rate continues, there will soon be more elderly than young people in country.*

Bulgaria has the lowest population growth of all countries in the EU. If this trend continues, by 2050 the population will have shrunk by as much as 35 per cent. To combat this, the government has begun encouraging people to have more children, but the campaign has not yet been successful.

Another reason for the population reduction is that many people are moving abroad. Between 1989 and 1995 around 800,000 Bulgarians moved abroad, mainly to other parts of Europe and to the USA. Even today many Bulgarians still move abroad – especially young people, because they feel there are better opportunities in other countries – although this number is slowly reducing.

Religion

The most popular religion is the Bulgarian Orthodox Church (about 83 per cent of people who follow a religion); around 13 per cent are Muslims, predominantly Turks and the Pomak – Bulgarians who have converted to Islam. There are also small groups of Roman Catholics, Protestants and Jews.

During the communist era, following a religion was not banned but was discouraged by the government. Religious instruction was forbidden and most people simply did not discuss their religious beliefs. Since the fall of communism in 1989, the Bulgarians are allowed to openly practise their religion and go to church or the mosque. Freedom of religion is part of the constitution.

For more than 15 years religion has been on the rise in Bulgaria, and religious books are extremely popular. Bulgarians are also quite superstitious, and are interested in ghosts and black magic.

▼ *The Russian Orthodox church in Sofia.*

Feast days and traditions

The Orthodox Christian religion is seen as the 'traditional' or national religion. The associated feast days are widely celebrated, especially Christmas and Easter. Even though not all Bulgarian Christians are church-goers, the churches are always filled at these times of year.

One Christmas tradition is *koleduvane*, in which young men go from house to house and sing Christmas songs. On New Year's Day Bulgarians have a feast and give each other presents. Children knock on doors and wish friends and family a Happy New Year. They carry a tree branch decorated with streamers, fruit and treats (*survachka*) with which they tap people on the shoulder in return for sweets and money.

▲ *The annual procession in Bansko. The men are playing traditional instruments, such as the gajda (a kind of bagpipe) and the kaval (a shepherd's pipe).*

National holidays are 3 March, which is Liberation Day, celebrating liberation from the Ottomans, and 24 May, when Bulgarians celebrate their culture and heritage.

A unique tradition is the celebration of *Baba Marta* ('Grandma March') on 1 March. This festival celebrates the change from winter to summer. *Baba Marta* has been celebrated since the creation of the First Bulgarian Empire in AD 681. On this day people give each other a *martenica*. *Martenici* (plural) are red and white tassels made of cotton or wool thread, which symbolise health, prosperity and happiness. Sometimes they are attached to small dolls, sometimes cherries. People wear them as bracelets or brooches. According to tradition they should be worn until the first stork or the first flowering tree – symbols of a new spring – have been seen. As soon as the wearer sees either of these signs, they hang their *martenica* on the branch of a fruit tree, which symbolises fertility. Sometimes, though, they are hidden under a rock, which is believed to drive out evil spirits.

Bulgarian yoghurt (*kiselo mljako*) is world famous. This dairy product contains a unique microbe called *Lactobacillus bulgaricus*, which gives the yoghurt a distinctive taste and it is thicker than the yoghurt typical in other parts of the world. *Kiselo mljako* has been enjoyed in the region for hundreds of years – even the Thracians ate it!

There are also many dishes that are made with cheese. Sirene is a typical Bulgarian cheese, white and salty, similar to feta cheese. Vegetarians can also choose from several thick vegetable soups. *Bob corba* (bean soup) is the best-known and can be bought everywhere. *Tarator* is a cold soup made from yoghurt, cucumber, garlic and dill. It also contains oil, water and walnuts. This is a favourite meal in summer, but it is also eaten as a starter all year round.

▲ *Meze.*

Meze **and** *rakija*

Meze are small snacks that are served with alcoholic drinks like *rakija*, a brandy made from distilled fermented fruit. *Rakija* is drunk all over the Balkans, although the fruit from which it is made varies from region to region. The Serbs use plums, for example, and the *rakija* is known as *slivovic*. Bulgarians use grapes as the basis; *rakija* distilled from grapes is known as *grozdova* or *grozdovica*. If the drink is made from Muscat grapes then it is called *muskatova*.

Bulgarians have a reputation for drinking a lot of alcohol, but drunks are not a common sight because Bulgarians eat *meze* and drink at the same time. Foods that often accompany *meze* are salads, different kinds of cheese and vegetables preserved in oil. Sausage is also very popular. The *lukanka* is a spicy salami with a strong flavour and Bulgarians also enjoy *sudžuk*, which is a sausage made from beef, similar to the Turkish *sucuk*. This can be quite mild or very spicy. Bread accompanies most meals in Bulgaria.

◀ Rakija *distillery.*

▲ *A glass of* rakija *and a glass of* ajrjan.

In Bulgaria it is quite common to sit at the table for over an hour and enjoy a couple of glasses of alcohol with *meze* before starting the main meal. The Bulgarians generally drink wine with their main course, but water or beer may also be served. Bulgarian wine, especially red wine, has gained a good reputation all over the world. The wines are strong, often made from Cabernet Sauvignon or Merlot grapes.

◀ Roast lamb is a favourite in Bulgaria, and is traditionally served on Saint George's Day – 6 May.

Meat dishes

Bulgarians like to eat their meat grilled. Lamb is the most popular, followed by pork. Sometimes there is wild boar on the menu. Favourite grilled meat dishes include *kebapceta* and *kjufteta*. *Kebapceta* are little rolls, *kjufteta* little balls of strongly seasoned minced meat. *Kavarma* is an everyday stew made from meat (mainly pork) and vegetables.

The evening meal is often soup and/or salad followed by grilled meat as a main course or a stew with potatoes. This may be followed by pudding such as *baklava*, a very sweet dish made from layers of puff pastry with honey and walnuts.

Bulgarian breakfast

Bulgarians love pies made from puff pastry. Pastries (sweet and savoury) can be bought at small stalls found on nearly every street corner. According to Bulgarians, the pastry known as *banica* is the most typical of Bulgarian foods. *Banica* is baked in the oven. It is made from beaten eggs and sirene (cheese) between layers of puff pastry, and variations have either spinach or a sweet filling. The cheese-filled kind is the most popular. Bulgarians don't take much time to eat breakfast. They usually just eat a piece of *banica* and drink a glass of *kiselo mljako* (which tranlates as sour milk, but is actually yoghurt) or *ajrjan* (a salty liquid yoghurt drink). They also drink *boza*, made from fermented millet or wheat. This is a thick, sweet liquid with a slightly sour taste, rather like cornflakes with milk. This is a particular favourite among children.

▼ A biscuit stall.

Very popular in Bulgaria, *sopska* salad is very easy to prepare. For four people you need 5 to 7 oz of spring onions or 1 big onion; 17 oz tomatoes; 5 to 7 oz ripe cheese (feta), grated or in small pieces; 1 green pepper and 1 red pepper; 1 small cucumber; 1 small pimento pepper; 2 large spoonfuls of oil and 1 large spoonful of vinegar; salt and pepper to taste.

Peel and dice the onion into small pieces. Chop the parsley very finely. Wash the tomatoes and cut them into small slices. Mix the onion, parsley and tomatoes. Peel the cucumber and cut it into pieces. Wash the peppers, remove the seeds and cut them into small pieces. Add the cucumber and peppers to the tomatoes. Pour oil and vinegar over the mixture and add salt and pepper to taste. Be careful when mixing the ingredients. Sprinkle the cheese over them together with the thin pimento pepper rings.

Economy

On 1 January 2007, Bulgaria and its neighbour Romania joined the European Union, marking a new era in the country's history.

Bulgarians consider this to be an important moment, because they have always thought of Bulgaria as a European country, despite the many years of Ottoman rule. Ten years previously, Bulgaria was in a deep economic crisis, but joining the EU brought new hope for recovery.

▲ *A lot of work still carried out using old equipment and materials, but here the horse and cart have been replaced.*

Bulgaria is slowly recovering from the worst of its economic problems thanks to widespread reform. However, the income and living standards of Bulgarians are still below that of other Europeans.

The economy under communism

Before the Second World War the Bulgarian economy was mainly based around agriculture, but this changed when the communists gained power in 1944 and began to industrialise the country. Agriculture was nationalised and collectivised according to the Soviet model. This meant that farmers had to give up all their land, and the state decided what and how much was to be grown; agriculture became a large-scale business instead of a small, family-led industry.

▼ *Women work the land.*

In any communist-led economy, the state determines supply and demand rather than the consumers (the citizens of that country). This means there is no competition in industry, and only items considered essential by the government were produced. During this time, Bulgaria only traded with other communist countries, but this meant there was always a market for the goods produced.

Towards a free market economy

This all changed with the fall of communism in 1989. Trade with Bulgaria's communist neighbours came to a standstill. The economy collapsed because the export market disappeared. The following years were extremely difficult for Bulgarians, as their incomes dropped considerably – and some were not even paid at all. Pensions were no longer paid and many people found themselves unemployed. There was not enough food and there was insufficient energy for electricity and other services. Many people found it hard just to survive day to day.

Bulgaria needed to become a free market economy – one in which supply and demand determined the market. This process took a long time, however, because the corrupt government was not keen on instigating such changes. Members of the government feared they would lose power and the opportunities for making themselves rich that the existing system offered. This resulted in a major economic crisis, but a new government began to turn the tide.

▲ Old people took a gloomy view of the future.

From 1997 onwards, large-scale reforms were carried out in Bulgaria. The currency (Lev) was tied to the German Mark and later the Euro. Inflation – which had been very high – dropped. The government privatised state enterprises and reformed the agricultural and energy sectors. These measures hit the people hard in the short term, but things began to improve as the economy slowly revitalised.

▶ As in most other countries, fast-food restaurants are popular.

Tourism

▲ *The beach at Varna.*

Under the communists, the Black Sea became a popular place for visitors from Eastern bloc countries to spend their holidays.

It is only in recent years that tourists from other countries have come to Bulgaria on holiday. In 2006 there were 5.2 million foreign tourists – twice the number there were in 2001.

Foreign tourists come mainly to visit the Black Sea coast, but holidaymakers also come to ski, to hike, and to admire the cultural heritage in places such as Plovdiv and Sofia.

▶ *The palace in Evksinograd.*

The beach and the Black Sea
Nearly three-quarters of all tourists come to Bulgaria to enjoy sun, sea and the beach. The Bulgarians themselves like to spend their holidays along the Black Sea coast, where there is a stretch of beach 160 km long. The two beach resorts are Varna in the north and Burgas in the south. Both towns have enormous tourist areas, including Sunny Beach and Golden Sands, where visitors can stay reasonably cheaply. However, such tourist spots do not offer a true taste of the country, so those wanting to see more typically Bulgarian sights visit Evksinograd, a former royal palace near Varna, or Nesebăr, a medieval town.

Winter sports
Bulgarians have long enjoyed winter sports in their country but it is only recently that foreign visitors have discovered sports such as skiing in Bulgaria. The mountains of the Pirin, Rila, Rodopi, Vitoša and the Balkans have many good ski resorts and pistes for all levels of skiers. The best time to go skiing, snowboarding or cross-country skiing is between November and March, when the snow is at its best.

The largest ski resorts are Borovec (in the Rila Mountains) and Pamporovo (in the Rodopi Mountains). Bansko is quite new but is already proving popular because of the stunning scenery – it is in the Pirin National Park – and good winter sports facilities.

◀ *Tourists enjoy the mountain scenery.*

◀ *The Snežanka Cave has beautiful stalactites and stalagmites.*

Hiking and mountain climbing

During the summer hiking or climbing in the same mountains are popular pastimes. More than one-third of Bulgaria is made up of mountains, so there are plenty of opportunities for climbing and hiking. Bulgarians are keen hikers and many travel to the high Balkan Mountains to indulge in this pastime. Not all the paths in the mountains are well-marked or passable, however, so they are not good for those who are inexperienced, and it is sensible to take a guide. The paths in the central part of the Balkan Mountains, between the Valley of the Roses and the Danube Lowlands, are passable. The Rodopi Mountains in the south are favourites with hikers and nature lovers. The varied scenery – rugged forests and Alpine meadows – are a beautiful sight. Bulgaria has three national parks: Pirin, Rila and Central Balkan National Park. Adventurous tourists enjoy trekking through the hundreds of caves scattered throughout Bulgaria.

Villages and towns

Sofia and Plovdiv both attract many tourists, but the most beautiful parts of Bulgaria are found in the countryside. In the mountains and the valleys such as Rila and Perin are villages and towns such as Bansko and Koprivštica, which retain an atmosphere of ancient times. Veliko Tărnovo, the medieval capital of the Second Bulgarian Empire, is typical of these towns – full of historical monuments such as the ruins of Carevec Castle. Several other forts can be found in the mountains.

Nesebăr

Nesebăr is an old fishing village on the Black Sea that was once an old harbour town. The houses in the old town are a treasure trove of architectural, historical and archaeological monuments from various periods, and much of it is very well-preserved. In Nesebăr, layer upon layer of different civilisations lie literally one on top of the other. The oldest archaeological layers date back more than 3,000 years. Nesebar is on UNESCO's World Heritage List. In summer the town is packed with people, but it is much quieter outside the tourist season. One of the most noticeable features here is the number of church ruins from the Byzantine, Bulgarian and Ottoman empires. The oldest ruins date from the fifth century.

▲ *The Orlov (Eagle) bridge in Sofia, designed by the Proseks, a Czech family of architects.*

▼ *Ruins in Nesebar.*

Glossary

Byzantine Empire the eastern part of the Roman Empire after it was divided in AD 395.

communism a political system in which all land and property are owned by the state.

constitution a set of principles by which a country is run. No laws can be passed that contradict these.

Cyrillic alphabet a system of writing based on the Greek alphabet and used in Slavic countries.

democracy a political system in which the people of a country choose who they wish to represent their interests in government.

Orthodox the Christian Church in the East; it has several independent sects.

propaganda information spread to further a particular cause.

sanctions fines that have to be paid for violating certain international laws.

Slavic relating to the Slavs, their culture or languages.

subjugated forced under the control of a stronger power, such as an invading army.

subsidies money paid by a government to help businesses that benefit the public.

Index